CHARLES B. & PATRICIA A.
TUBBS
CHILDREN'S
LIBRARY

Profiles in American History

*The Life and Times of*

# JOHN PAUL JONES

Mitchell Lane
PUBLISHERS

P.O. Box 196 · Hockessin, Delaware 19707

# Profiles in American History

## Titles in the Series

*The Life and Times of*

Abigail Adams
Alexander Hamilton
Benjamin Franklin
Betsy Ross
Eli Whitney
George Rogers Clark
Hernando Cortés
John Adams
John Cabot
John Hancock
John Paul Jones
John Peter Zenger
Nathan Hale
Patrick Henry
Paul Revere
Peter Stuyvesant
Samuel Adams
Sir Walter Raleigh
Stephen F. Austin
Susan B. Anthony
Thomas Jefferson
William Penn

Profiles in American History

*The Life and Times of*

# JOHN PAUL JONES

Susan Sales Harkins and
William H. Harkins

Printed and bound in the United States of America.

Printing 1 2 3 4 5 6 7 8 9

Library of Congress Cataloging-in-Publication Data
Harkins, Susan Sales.
The life and times of John Paul Jones / by Susan Sales Harkins and William H. Harkins.
p. cm. — (Profiles in American history)
Includes bibliographical references and index.
Audience: Grades 7-8.
ISBN 978-1-58415-529-4 (library bound)
1. Jones, John Paul, 1747–1792—Juvenile literature. 2. Admirals—United States—Biography—Juvenile literature. 3. United States. Navy—Biography—Juvenile literature. 4. United States—History—Revolution, 1775–1783—Naval operations—Juvenile literature. I. Harkins, William H. II. Title.
E207.J7H19 2008
973.3'5092—dc22
[B]

2007000794

**ABOUT THE AUTHOR'S:** Susan and William Harkins live in Kentucky, where they enjoy writing together for children. Susan has written many books for adults and children. William is a history buff. In addition to writing, he is a member of the Air National Guard.

**PHOTO CREDITS:** Cover—Stock Montage/Getty Images; pp. 1, 3, 24—Library of Congress; pp. 6, 12, 22—U.S. National Archives and Records Administration; pp. 11, 27, 30, 34—North Wind Picture Archives; pp. 16, 42—Naval Historical Center; p. 35—Jonathan Scott; p. 32—Superstock.

**PUBLISHER'S NOTE:** This story is based on the authors' extensive research, which they believe to be accurate. Documentation of such research is contained on page 47.

The internet sites referenced herein were active as of the publication date. Due to the fleeting nature of some web sites, we cannot guarantee they will all be active when you are reading this book.

PLB

# Profiles in American History

## Contents

*John Paul Jones, though a small man, had no trouble commanding the respect of his men and his enemies. For that reason, artists tend to portray him as "bigger than life." He was fond of flashy clothes and even designed his own naval uniform.*

# CHAPTER 1

## A Moonlit Victory

Captain Richard Pearson scanned the wake from HMS *Serapis* as the frigate glided over the glassy water. Behind her, forty-one merchant ships of all sizes filled the horizon. The British convoy the *Serapis* escorted was still three days from London, and from safety.

So far, the trip from Denmark had been uneventful. Perhaps it had been *too* easy, Pearson thought.

The captain looked toward the English coast for a red flag, the signal that the enemy was close. No British merchant ship was safe from Yankee privateers since the war with the thirteen colonies had begun.

He glanced toward the HMS *Countess of Scarborough*. The smaller ship, a 20-gun sloop of war, was helping him protect the convoy. In these troubled times, it paid to have as much firepower as possible.

North of Scarborough Castle, he spotted the first flag. Soon a warning letter arrived by rowboat from shore. The American pirate John Paul Jones had been spotted nearby with four ships.

No one had to tell the captain who John Paul Jones was. That scoundrel had raided Whitehaven a year earlier, in 1778. He was the first enemy in one hundred years with the guts and bravado to invade England. Every captain in the Royal Navy wanted a chance to take revenge on Jones.

Pearson had confidence in the *Serapis*. She was one of the newest ships in the British Royal Navy. Her copper bottom made her faster than anything else in the water. With fifty guns spanning two decks, she was terrifying in battle. He knew that the *Serapis* was superior to whatever Jones was sailing.

However, Pearson wasn't facing only Jones—he was facing a small fleet. With thirty years in the Royal Navy, he had enough experience to know that the odds were against him. There were no other British warships in the area to help. It would be just his *Serapis* and the *Countess of Scarborough* against at least four enemy ships with far more gun power. Pearson ordered the convoy to sail for the coast.

Later that afternoon, Pearson called all hands to battle stations. Two drummers marched the length of the ship, sounding the alarm. Crewmen secured the ship's sails. Below deck, a surgeon prepared for the wounded.

Then the captain sailed straight for Jones and the *Bonhomme Richard*. Most likely, Jones would be the victor, but the battle would give the convoy a chance to escape.

Meanwhile, Commodore Jones was busy stalking his next prize—one of the convoy's merchant ships. Dressed in a blue-and-white uniform of his own design, he slowly closed the gap between the *Bonhomme Richard* and his prey. At thirty-two, Jones was smaller than his officers, but he was athletic and well built. Despite his short stature, he was the picture of confidence standing straight in his striking uniform.

The *Bonhomme Richard* was the largest ship Jones had commanded. It had originally been a merchant ship. With sixty tons of armament on deck, she was slower than the British *Serapis* and hard to handle. Confined in the hold were nearly a hundred English prisoners, taken from captured ships.

Her crew was another disadvantage. About one third of them were Americans. Many were French sailors. Some were even captured Englishmen, who preferred to fight for the United States rather than languish in prison. Rounding out the crew were a few Portuguese and Scandinavian sailors. Many of the crewmen had little or even no experience as seamen. Many didn't understand English.

Near six o'clock that evening, drums summoned Jones's crew to battle stations. He signaled the fleet's next largest ships, the *Alliance* and the *Pallas*, to form a line of battle. Together, the three ships would sail past the *Serapis*, each taking broadside shots as they passed. The first ship would likely take return fire from the *Serapis*, but the British wouldn't have time to reload before the second and third ships passed by.

Jones's plan gave the Americans the upper hand, but within minutes everything changed. Captain Pierre Landais of the *Alliance* failed to obey Jones's order and headed for open sea. Then the *Pallas* also altered course, sailing away from the *Serapis* and engaging the *Countess of Scarborough*. The fleet's remaining ship, the twelve-gun *Vengeance*, was too small to take on the *Serapis*. The *Bonhomme Richard* was on its own.

Had the captains on the other ships in Jones's fleet obeyed his orders, the Americans could have easily taken the *Serapis*. However, in a one-on-one battle, the *Bonhomme Richard* was no match for the British ship.

By seven o'clock the full moon was rising and the sea was calm. In the fading light, the *Serapis* called to the *Bonhomme Richard* to identify itself. On the third hail, Jones replied by lowering his ship's British ensign, raising the American colors, and then firing on the *Serapis*.

At almost the same moment, the *Serapis* fired. Then a second round from both ships met their targets, followed by a small explosion aboard the *Bonhomme Richard*. Two of her eighteen-pounder guns had exploded when they were fired, damaging the ship and killing several crewmen. Now it was feared that the ship's other eighteen-pounders were unsafe, so they were taken out of service. The *Serapis* fired a third broadside shot that killed twenty marines aboard the *Bonhomme Richard*.

Jones knew his ship was in danger of being destroyed by the powerful guns of the *Serapis*. He had two options: make a run for it or board the *Serapis*. To board the enemy ship, Jones would have to sail the *Bonhomme Richard* alongside the *Serapis*. It was risky, but at such close range, the guns on the *Serapis* would be useless.

Meanwhile, Pearson knew he had to keep the *Bonhomme Richard* at a distance, where he could blow her out of the water with his long-range guns.

Jones brought the *Bonhomme Richard* alongside the *Serapis*. Dodging musket fire and grenades, the crew of the *Bonhomme Richard* tried to use grappling hooks to grab the British ship. The attempt failed.

Jones steered his ship left to right in front of the *Serapis*. Pearson swung the *Serapis* to the left, but it still hit the back end of the American ship. The ships were now side by side, but headed in opposite directions.

Jones grabbed a broken line from the *Serapis* and secured it to the *Bonhomme Richard*. With the riggings of both ships hopelessly ensnared, Jones ordered his men to tie the two vessels together with strong cables.

Both ships continued to fire their big guns at point-blank range.

They'd been at full battle for an hour when Captain Thomas Piercy of the *Countess of Scarborough* moved in to take broadside shots at the *Bonhomme Richard*. He found the smoke so heavy and the ships so close that he couldn't distinguish one ship from the other.

Two hours into the battle, the *Alliance* sailed back into the action. Jones thought Captain Landais planned to board the *Serapis* from the other side. Instead, Landais steered the *Alliance* to within fifty yards of the two entangled ships and began to fire—not once, but three times. The broadside assault killed many men aboard the *Bonhomme Richard*. It also took out several guns on that side of the ship. Landais had fired upon the wrong ship!

Sometime during the next two hours, a rumor spread through the lower deck of the *Bonhomme Richard*. The ship was sinking and the captain was dead!

Around ten o'clock, Jones was surprised to hear someone from his ship surrender: "Quarter! Quarter! For God's sake, quarter!"

Jones pulled a pistol from his belt and ran toward the voice. He found Henry Gardner at the railing, waving a lantern high above his head to guide the crew of the *Serapis*. At that same moment, Gardner saw his captain—alive! Only then did Gardner realize his mistake. The captain raised his pistol and pulled the trigger, but it was empty.

*The battle between the* Serapis *and the* Bonhomme Richard. *Mistakes were made during the battle for the British* Serapis. *Despite the odds, Jones refused to give up, and in the end, he won the battle.*

There wasn't time to reload, so he threw the empty pistol at Gardner. It struck the back of Gardner's skull as he tried to escape. He fell to the deck.

On the *Serapis*, Pearson had heard the cry of surrender. He shouted over the battle to Jones, "Sir, do you ask for quarter?"

"No sir!" Jones shouted back. "I do not ask for quarter."

A moment later, the tired Jones shouted over the din of battle his famous words, "I have not yet begun to fight!"[1]

Near ten-thirty, a thunderous crash startled the crews of both ships when the mainmast on the *Serapis* cracked and fell. With his ship out of commission, Captain Pearson surrendered the *Serapis* to Commodore Jones.

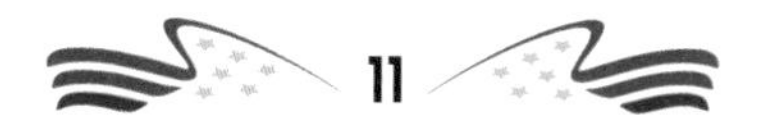

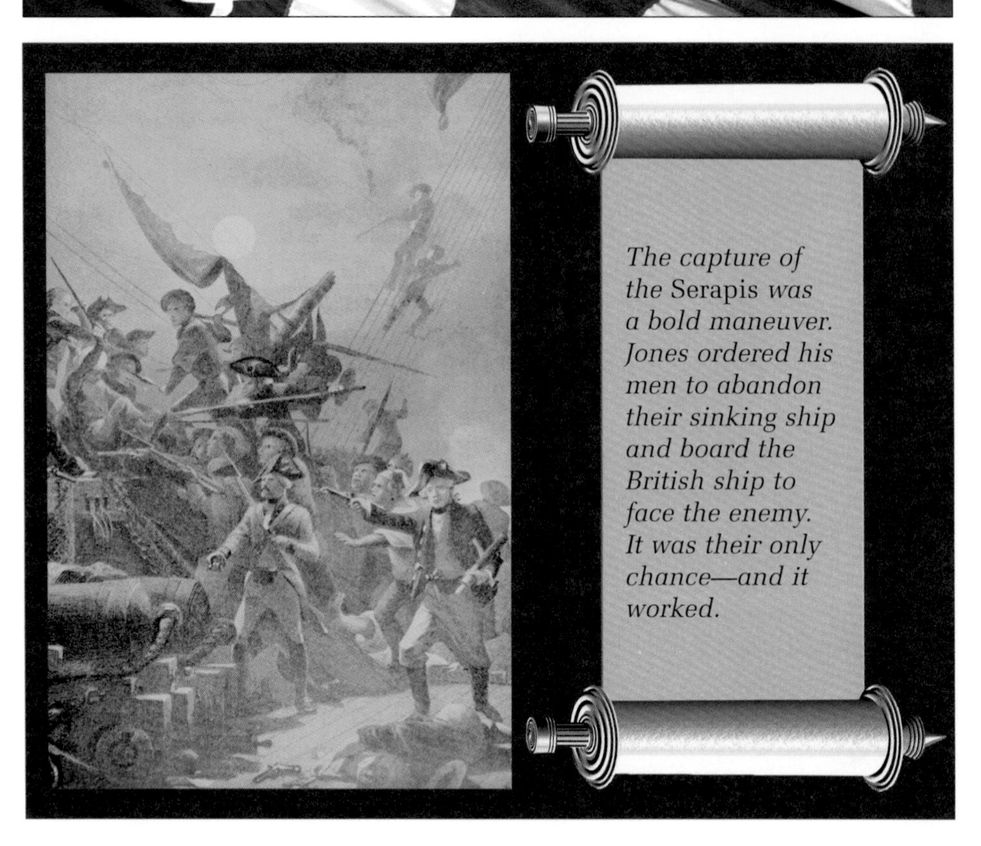

*The capture of the* Serapis *was a bold maneuver. Jones ordered his men to abandon their sinking ship and board the British ship to face the enemy. It was their only chance—and it worked.*

Meanwhile, during their own battle, the *Pallas* had overwhelmed the *Countess of Scarborough*.

It was late the next day when Jones finally transferred his command to the *Serapis*. From the deck of the captured ship, the captains and crews watched the fatally wounded *Bonhomme Richard* sink into the dark bubbling water. The battle was over. Jones had two new prize ships, but he'd lost the *Bonhomme Richard*.

In a report to Benjamin Franklin in Paris, Jones accused Landais of criminal conduct, cowardice, dereliction of duty, and treason. Eventually, the navy dismissed Landais as unfit for command, but they never tried him in court.

Politically, the victory was a success for Jones. Even citizens of Great Britain thought him a hero. Pearson remained a prisoner of war until 1780, when he returned home a national hero.

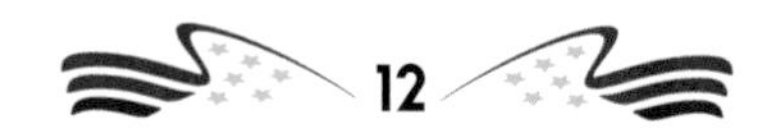

## What Jones Really Said

Historians disagree as to whether Jones actually made the statement for which he's so famous: "I have not yet begun to fight!" When the exchange occurred, Jones was in trouble. His ship was slowly sinking. Pearson called to him over the battle, asking if he wished for quarter (to surrender). Jones wrote in his official report that he responded negatively, but he didn't share his actual words.

*Richard Dale*

Richard Dale was one of Jones's lieutenants on the *Bonhomme Richard*. Many years after the battle, he was the first to share Jones's response publicly. He told a biographer that Jones had shouted, "I have not yet begun to fight!" That remark certainly fit the battle scene.

In his memoirs, Jones quoted himself in French: *Je ne songe point à me rendre, mais je suis determiné à vous faire demander quartier*. Translated, that means, "I haven't as yet thought of surrendering, but I am determined to make you ask for quarter."[2]

It seems unlikely that a man in the midst of battle would take the time and energy to make such a long response. Some historians speculate that in later years, Jones hoped to improve what he actually said. He may have felt his succinct, though defiant and very appropriate, comment wasn't lofty enough for the occasion. It's also possible that he didn't remember what he actually said and tried to document the essence of his response.

We do know that Jones often exaggerated and embellished his participation in events. His memoirs and letters are written in a lavish and flamboyant style—one that was very popular in his day. It's easy to imagine that he actually made the curt and rapid reply for which he's famous. Later, instead of appreciating the elegant statement, he may have found it lacking.

*The* Bonhomme Richard *sinking*

*Jones cut a dashing figure in his naval uniform. At parties, women thought him handsome and charming.*

## Childhood Adventures, Troubles, and a Mystery

John Paul grew up in a world of contrasts. His father, John Paul, was the head gardener for a huge Scottish estate named Arbigland. Over one hundred servants, including John's mother, Jean McDuff, kept the house and estates in order. Because he was the head gardener, the servants on the estate treated John Paul Sr. with respect. In contrast, the Earl of Selkirk, the estate's owner, cared little for the gardener's expertise and advice.

The sting of disparity between master and servant haunted John Paul his entire life. It probably began with his father. It made no difference to the earl that John Paul Sr. was an expert in his trade. The gardener was his servant, not his equal. At that time, social position determined everything, and the smart servant kept his or her place. Paul would fight his entire life to shed his humble roots.

Born on July 6, 1747, John was the youngest of five children born to John and Jean Paul. (John Paul would add the name Jones as an adult.) Gardening was the Paul family's business. John's grandfather owned a combination tavern and market garden.

From the family's cramped two-room cottage, John had a spectacular view of the Firth of Solway (the channel that separates Scotland and England). On a clear day, he could see the English coast. Sitting on his front lawn, he watched huge ships sail up and down the

*John Paul Jones was born in Scotland on July 6, 1747. He and his family lived in a small gardener's cottage of the Arbigland estate on the shores of the Solway Firth.*

firth. John spent his childhood breathing salt air and playing in the estate's beautiful gardens.

John often went into town and listened to the sailors tell stories of the sea and America. He had a small sailboat, and he spent a lot of time fishing and playing admiral.

The boy received a solid education in a parish school at Kirkbean. He hoped to join the Royal Navy, as noted in a letter to Benjamin Franklin years later: "I had made the art of war at sea in some degree my study, and had been fond of the navy, from boyish days up."[1] Unfortunately, John didn't have the right social connections.

Instead of joining the navy, John began an apprenticeship to an English merchant. At the age of thirteen, he went to sea aboard the merchant ship *Friendship*.

Life on a merchant ship was quite a change for him. He left a small wholesome home surrounded by dense woods and fragrant gardens, where fresh milk and vegetables were abundant. Aboard the *Friendship*, he lived below deck. It stank of unwashed men, human waste, vomit, and putrid seawater. He ate salt beef and dried peas for every meal. Even though he was only thirteen, John received half a pint of rum or a half-gallon of beer every day. Unlike most seamen, John never learned to drink hard liquor, not even the free rum.

Life at sea was exhausting and dangerous, but John became a good sailor. Over the next four years, he learned all that he could about sailing. Captain Benson of the *Friendship* taught John how to navigate using an octant. It was an unusual decision for the captain. Officers didn't teach ordinary seaman to navigate, but the captain saw something special in John. Later, knowing how to navigate would change John's life.

Then, quite unexpectedly, John found himself unemployed. The owner of the *Friendship* sold his ship and released Paul from his apprenticeship. Work was hard to find. John ended up on a slave ship, the *King George*. Two years later, he advanced to first mate on another slave ship, the *Two Friends*. We don't know how John felt about his time on the two slavers, but in 1767, he quit the *Two Friends* before securing a new position.

A Scottish captain, Samuel McAdam, offered John a ride to Scotland. On the voyage, both Captain McAdam and the first mate died of fever. Because John knew how to navigate, he was able to sail the ship home. He saved the ship, its cargo, and its crew. The owner was so grateful that he gave John command of the ship, even though he was only twenty-one years old.

Young Captain Paul was demanding, but his crew seemed to do well under his command—at least at first. He often clashed with those who failed to show him the proper respect as their captain. No one ever described Paul as easygoing.

On his second voyage, his carpenter's mate was a man named Mungo Maxwell. The carpenter came from a prominent family.

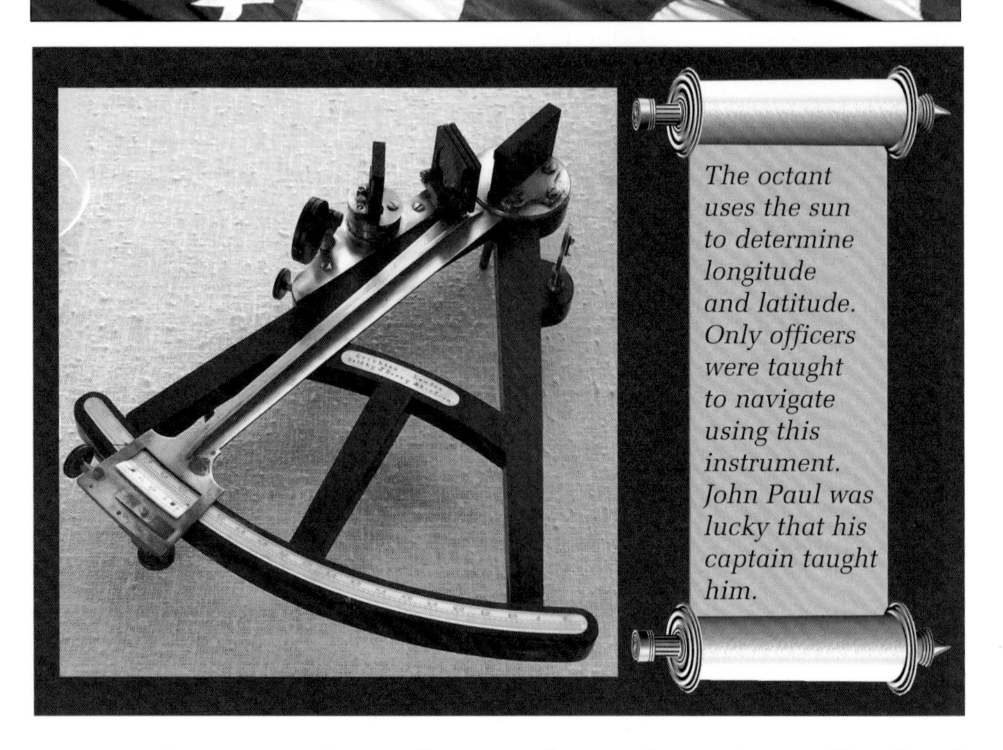

*The octant uses the sun to determine longitude and latitude. Only officers were taught to navigate using this instrument. John Paul was lucky that his captain taught him.*

Because Captain Paul was the son of a gardener, Maxwell refused to obey his orders. Eventually, Maxwell's behavior led to a flogging. Maxwell sued Captain Paul for the insult, but a court in Tobago ruled that the captain's actions were justified. Harsh treatment wasn't unusual during those times. Captains had absolute power aboard their ships. Captain Paul won the case, but the victory was short-lived.

Maxwell quit the *John* and returned to Scotland on another ship. Meanwhile, Paul sailed the *John* home. He was shocked to find himself under arrest when he docked. Maxwell had died at sea, and his family wanted vengeance.

Paul returned to the Caribbean to gather evidence of his innocence. Among that evidence was a statement from the captain of the ship on which Maxwell had died. According to this captain, James Eastment, Maxwell boarded the ship in good health. At sea, he caught a fever and died. In addition, Paul collected papers from the civil case in Tobago that cleared him of any crime in the flogging incident. The Scottish court reviewed Paul's evidence and dismissed the case.

In 1772, Paul took command of the *Betsy*. In those days, the captains of merchant ships received a percentage of the profits. Paul saved his money. Someday, he hoped to buy a small plantation in Virginia. He was on his way to leaving his servant roots behind and becoming a gentleman.

Then, he fell ill. While recuperating, a load of butter sitting aboard the *Betsy* spoiled. Instead of paying his sailors in advance, as he usually did, he bought new cargo. Once he sold the cargo in London, he would pay his men. While it wasn't the best way to do business, it wasn't that unusual. Unfortunately for Paul, one of his sailors objected. We don't know the sailor's name; Captain Paul referred to him only as "the Ringleader"[2] in his writings. The Ringleader called for mutiny. When he tried to take control of the ship, he threatened Paul with a large wooden club. The captain clasped his sword in his hand and tried to retreat. The Ringleader lunged forward to strike the captain and fell on the captain's sword. The death was an accident, according to Paul. He turned himself in to the authorities in Tobago, even though it was legal for a captain to kill a mutinous sailor.

At that time, Tobago was the property of the British crown. Normally, the Admiralty Court would have heard Paul's case. As luck would have it, the Admiralty Court wasn't in session. A local Tobagan court would hear his case, and that was bad news for Paul. The Ringleader was a local. Although an Englishman, he lived in Tobago.

The Admiralty Court would have exonerated Captain Paul. A local court wouldn't be so predictable. Archibald Stuart, Paul's business partner at the time, advised him to flee to America. Stuart would send him money. When the Admiralty Court was back in session, Paul could return to face any charges. Paul took Stuart's advice. No one knows how Paul made his way to America. He didn't write about the trip in his memoirs.

Paul found himself a stranger in America, with no money. It appears that his business partner double-crossed him. Stuart never sent Paul any money. Nor did Paul ever hear from him again. Before Paul could return to Tobago, the American Revolution started.

His first year in America was difficult. Paul knew no one. Once again, he faced the disparity of social status. Despite his accomplishments at sea, he was still the son of a gardener. Even worse, he was Scottish. The Virginian gentry were English and looked down on the Scots who lived to the west of Virginia's coastal towns.

It was during this time that John Paul became John Paul Jones. We don't know why he took a new name or why he chose Jones. Most likely, he wanted to hide his identity, at least until he could clear himself in Tobago. Perhaps he decided not to return to Tobago and wanted a fresh start. Since Jones left no explanation of his own, we can only speculate.

Soon, the Freemasons befriended him. (The Freemasons are a secret and fraternal society.) Jones was a mason, and the society took care of their own. In particular, Jones spent a lot of time with Dr. John Read, a mason and a fellow Scotsman. Dr. Read was generous with his home and his library. Jones began to read—a lot. He hoped to improve his mind. More than anything else, he wanted to be a gentleman.

On Dr. Read's estate, Jones waited as the American colonists prepared for war. He saw the rebellion as an opportunity. Toward the end of 1775, Jones traveled to Philadelphia to enlist in the navy, which didn't exist yet. He had no other prospects for employment and no loving family to leave behind. In short, he had nothing to lose. Most likely, the Continental Navy saved Jones from a life of obscurity and poverty.

*John Paul Jones statue, Potomac, Maryland*

## Society-Crossed Lovers

While spending time with a fellow mason, Dr. Read, Jones met and fell in love with Dr. Read's neighbor, Dorothea Spottswood Dandridge.

*Alexander Spottswood*

Dorothea came from a distinguished family in Hanover County, Virginia. Her grandfather, Alexander Spottswood, was a colonial governor. Her family ran a prosperous and luxurious plantation. Patriots visited her family on a regular basis. In fact, George Washington's wife, Martha, was Dorothea's cousin.

Dorothea was a dark-haired, dark-eyed beauty. At nineteen, she was ready to marry. We don't know how serious about one another Dorothea and Jones were. Jones was determined to become a landowner in Virginia. Marrying into Virginia society was certainly one way to satisfy that goal.

Jones wrote very little about the affair, other than to mention that he gave up love to go to war. The truth is, Jones was beneath Dorothea socially. There was never any real hope for a marriage between the two. Dorothea's family would have never allowed her to marry Jones.

*Dorothea Spottswood*

Dr. Read wrote to Jones in 1777 about Dorothea's marriage to Patrick Henry, America's famous orator and the Commonwealth of Virginia's first governor: "Miss Dandridge is no more, that is, she a few months ago gave herself into the arms of Patrick Henry."[3]

It does appear that there's some truth to the love story. One Henry biographer gave some credence to the story: ". . . neighborhood gossip held that Dolly had fancied an impecunious young sailor named John Paul Jones, then visiting cousins on a nearby plantation, but her father dashed her hopes in favor of the more glorious match with the governor."[4]

Jones had many love affairs, but never married.

For Your Information

*John Paul Jones entered the Continental Navy as an officer aboard the Alfred. Before long, he had a ship of his own, the Providence.*

# CHAPTER 3

## A Revolutionary Sea Captain

In 1775, the British Navy was the strongest naval force in the world. With 270 ships, they were used to winning. In contrast, the American colonies had no ships at all.

Protecting her shores from British attacks was a problem. While the Naval Committee planned to build frigates, Lord Dunmore, the British governor of Virginia, was attacking the coast. He seized merchant ships and raided coastal villages.

The colonists needed ships right away. In December of 1775, the committee began adding cannons to merchant ships.

Even with a few ships, the new Continental Navy was no challenge to the British. The new officers and seamen were ill prepared to take on the greatest navy in the world. In fact, most of the early captains, officers, and sailors were incompetent.

To fill posts, the Naval Committee turned to friends and family. The committee put Esek Hopkins in charge of the entire fleet. Hopkins's brother was Stephen Hopkins, the committee's chairman. To captain the largest ship, the *Alfred*, they chose Dudley Saltonstall. He was the brother-in-law of Silas Deane, another committee member. Many men with family and social connections to the Naval Committee received commissions despite their lack of experience.

*When the colonies declared their independence from England, the British governor of Virginia, Lord Dunmore, escaped aboard a British warship. For months, he attacked small settlements along the shores of the Chesapeake Bay.*

A fellow Freemason recommended Jones to Joseph Hewes, a member of the Naval Committee. Hewes offered Jones command of the *Providence*, but Jones turned it down. She was tricky and dangerous to handle. He simply didn't feel confident enough to sail her.

On December 7, 1775, First Lieutenant Jones boarded the *Alfred*. She had thirty guns on her upper deck, which made her tip to either side. Merchant ships didn't haul heavy cannons well.

Despite makeshift ships and inexperienced officers, the new navy headed for open sea on January 3, 1776. A band played and a large crowd cheered. Lieutenant Jones thought the Americans had

gone mad. Did the Congress really mean to engage the British navy? Later, he would write to his friend and mentor Robert Morris about that day: "Was it proof of madness in the first corps of sea officers to have at so critical a period launched out on the ocean with only two armed merchant ships, two armed brigantines, and one armed sloop, to make war against such power as Great Britain?"[1]

The small fleet seemed doomed from the start. First, ice on the Delaware River slowed its progress. While the sailors waited for the ice to melt, smallpox broke out. Men began to desert before the mission had even begun.

Jones used the extra time to train his men. Most of them had no experience handling big guns. Jones knew that the British gun crews were the fastest in the world. If he and his men had any hope of holding their own in battle, they would need lots of practice.

Three more sloops joined the small fleet in mid-February. Their mission from Congress was to find and destroy Lord Dunmore and then clear the coasts of British warships.

Despite orders, Commodore Hopkins never even looked for Lord Dunmore. Low on men because of the smallpox, he headed for the Bahamas in search of gunpowder.

A storm caught the ships just two days out to sea. The strong winds blew two ships, the *Hornet* and the *Fly*, into one another. Then they seemed to disappear into the storm. Later, the fleet learned that the damaged sloops had returned to port.

On March 1, the fleet was sailing in the warm waters of the Caribbean. The men seized a couple of fishing schooners, but their prize wasn't fish, or even the boats. They learned from the sailors on the schooners that the British were storing gunpowder at New Providence Island in the Bahamas.

According to his memoirs, Jones devised a plan to seize the gunpowder. In February, the fleet landed on a small island several miles from New Providence. From there, they mounted an attack.

The island wasn't prepared for the attack, and Fort Montagne fell quickly. However, the cocky marines took a nap, giving the governor of the island the chance to move most of the gunpowder. Among the spoils, the marines seized seventy-eight cannons and fifteen mortars. They also collected more than sixteen thousand shells and cannonballs. They found only twenty barrels of gunpowder—the few the governor was unable to remove. (Sources disagree on the exact amount of munitions captured, but they do agree that the marines found very little gunpowder.)

Jones's memoirs claim that he was responsible for the plan. Commodore Hopkins didn't credit Jones in his official report. The marines headed home with their spoils.

Over a month later, just twenty miles south of Narragansett Bay in Rhode Island, a lookout spotted a British warship by moonlight. It was one-thirty in the morning on April 6. The sea was calm and the weather was warm.

By two o'clock that morning, the *Alfred* was ready for battle. The sleepy sailors waited at their posts. Most of them had never been in a sea battle.

No signal came from Hopkins. Instead, the commodore let the captains determine how they would engage the enemy ship, the *Glasgow*. When the *Glasgow* came within hailing distance, a marine aboard Hopkins's flagship, the *Cabot*, threw a hand grenade onto the deck of the *Glasgow*. The battle was on. It is unclear whether the marine acted on orders or on his own.

The British ship responded with broadside shots into the *Cabot*, wounding Hopkins and disabling his ship. Next, the *Glasgow* targeted the *Alfred*. Jones was belowdecks with the small gunners. A powerful shot from the *Glasgow* put the *Alfred* out of commission for several minutes.

The *Andrew Doria* couldn't maneuver around the other American ships to take clear aim at the *Glasgow*. The *Columbus* managed to bump the British ship. The *Providence* didn't even attempt to engage the British enemy ship.

With a hole in her hull, and a damaged rigging and sails, the *Glasgow* retreated. She got away.

The first sea battle in the history of the United States Navy was a failure. Had Hopkins called for a combined assault, the *Glasgow* wouldn't have stood a chance.

After a short investigation, the Naval Committee convicted the captain of the *Providence* for stealing and other crimes. The committee offered the ship to Jones. He accepted and took command on

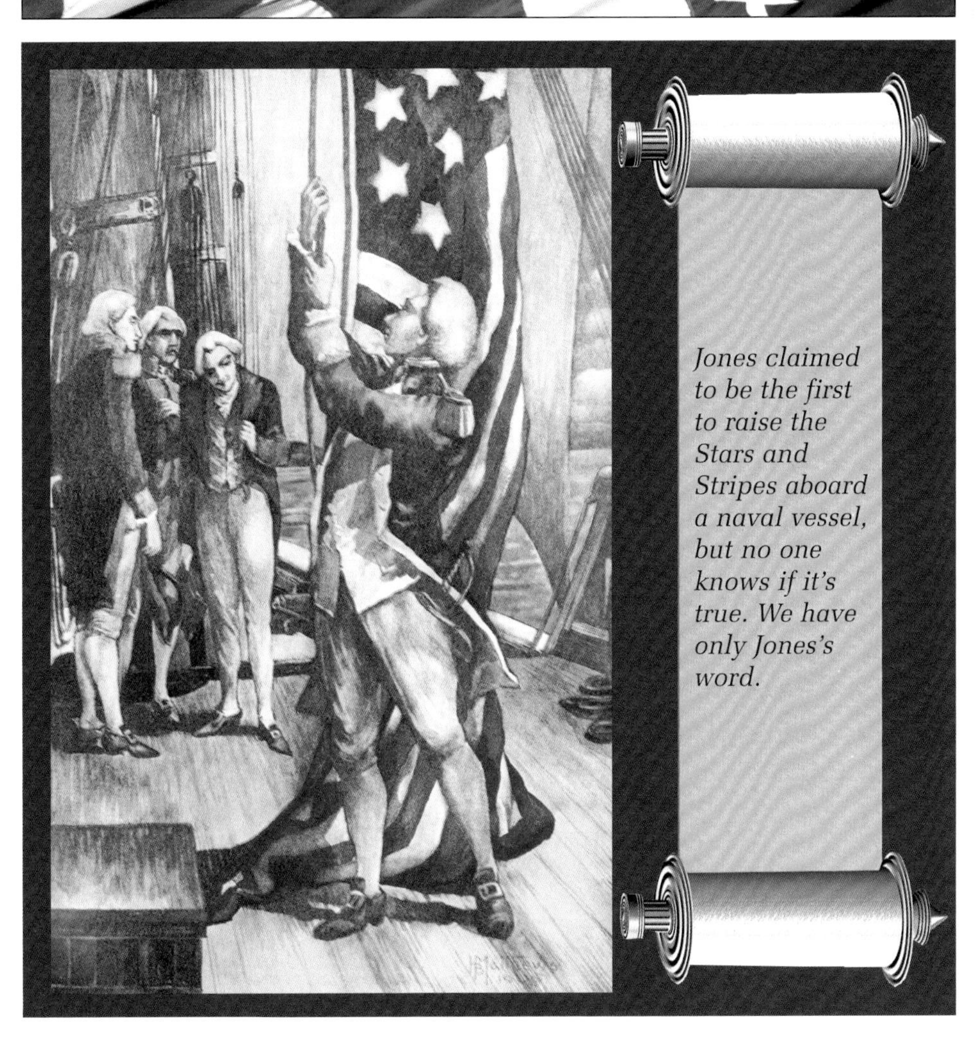

*Jones claimed to be the first to raise the Stars and Stripes aboard a naval vessel, but no one knows if it's true. We have only Jones's word.*

May 10, 1776. Congress issued and signed the official document on October 10. In January of 1777, the committee dismissed Hopkins from the navy.

Captain Jones quickly learned to love the *Providence*. She required special care to avoid capsizing in heavy winds, but she was fast. That made her perfect for the cat-and-mouse game for which Jones became famous. He would approach a British ship and remain just out of gun range, taunting the captain. When the enemy vessel finally gave chase, Jones would sail just out of range for hours and then suddenly vanish.

When he wasn't teasing British sea captains, he was enjoying Philadelphia's society. Most men found the young captain boastful, but the ladies found him charming.

On July 4, the Continental Congress declared independence from England by signing the Declaration of Independence. In answer to the rebellion, the British sailed 130 ships into New York's harbor.

With the enemy occupying an American harbor, Jones sailed the *Providence* south, to the Bahamas. There, he hoped to seize British merchant ships, which the navy could press into service. As captain, Jones would receive ten percent from the sale of all confiscated cargo. He hoped to purchase a small plantation and become part of the gentry.

On August 26, the *Providence* encountered HMS *Solebay*. Weather conditions weren't right for a quick getaway and the *Solebay* came dangerously close. The *Solebay* raised an American flag, trying to trick Jones. The trick didn't work.

Just as the *Solebay* prepared to fire on the *Providence*, Jones changed course, cutting right in front of the British ship. The new position gave Jones the wind he needed to leave the *Solebay* far behind. It was a bold move and it earned him the respect of his crew—at least for a while.

Jones and his crew returned home in October after seizing sixteen British ships.

IN CONGRESS.

The DELEGATES of the UNITED STATES of *New-Hampshire Maſſachuſetts-Bay; Rhode-Iſland, Connecticut, New-York New-Jerſey, Pennſylvania, Delaware, Maryland, Virginia, North-Carolina; South-Carolina,* and *Georgia,* TO

*John Paul Jones, Esquire,*

WE, repoſing eſpecial Truſt and Confidence in your Patriotiſm, Valour, Conduct, and Fidelity, DO, by theſe Preſents, conſtitute and appoint you to be *Captain* ~~of the armed ——— called the~~ ——— in the ~~Service~~ *Navy* of the United States of North-America, fitted out for the Defence of American Liberty, and for repelling every hoſtile invaſion thereof. You are therefore carefully and diligently to diſcharge the Duty of *Captain* ——— by doing and performing all manner of Things thereunto belonging. And we do ſtrictly charge and require all Officers, Marines and Seamen under your Command, to be obedient to your Orders as *Captain* And you are to obſerve and follow ſuch Orders and Directions from Time to Time as you ſhall receive from this or a future Congreſs of the United States, or Committee of Congreſs for that Purpoſe appointed, or Commander in Chief for the Time being of the Navy of the United States or any other your ſuperior Officer, according to the Rules and Diſcipline of War, the Uſage of the Sea and the Inſtructions herewith given you, in Purſuance of the Truſt repoſed in you. This Commiſſion to continue in Force until revoked by this or a future Congreſs.

DATED at *Philadelphia, October 10th 1776.*

By Order of the CONGRESS,

*John Hancock* PRESIDENT.

ATTEST. *Chas Thomson secy*

## *Providence*

Jones's first command in the Continental Navy was aboard the *Providence.* His seventy-three officers and men were crammed aboard the seventy-foot sloop. Cramped quarters were normal, and the men didn't complain.

Below deck, the men slept in hammocks. Officially, each crewman had just fourteen inches, from side to side, for his hammock. The men were practically sleeping on top of each other. The only air came through the open hatchway.

Twenty-five marines were also onboard. The marines acted as a small police force, and had no sailing responsibilities. They slept between the sailors and the officers. This arrangement protected the officers from any angry sailors. One marine stood at attention outside the captain's cabin at all times. The captain's cabin was a small chamber. There was barely room for his bed and a small desk and chair. He did have one luxury—a window.

With only twelve guns on board, she wasn't much of a match against the British warships. In combat, the *Providence* was effective only as part of a larger fleet. If captured, the crew could expect to spend the war in a British prison. If they were lucky, the British would exchange them for British prisoners of war. As a Scotsman, however, Jones was a British subject. If he were caught, the British would hang him as a traitor.

*The* Providence

*An eager John Paul Jones raided the home of the Earl of Selkirk, hoping to kidnap the earl. British authorities were horrified when they learned of the raid.*

# CHAPTER 4

## In Enemy Waters

While Jones was playing cat and mouse in the Atlantic, on old merchant ships outfitted with a few guns, Congress was building new warships. Jones was impatient to prove himself. He wanted one of those new ships. He thought he was one of the best captains in the Continental Navy.

Congress didn't agree. They rewarded American officers. Jones was Scottish, not American. Besides, members of Congress and the Naval Committee, which had renamed itself the Marine Committee, found Jones to be annoying. They were tired of getting letter after letter from Jones complaining about everything and giving advice. Jones longed for recognition and acceptance. He never got it.

Finally, in November of 1776, Captain Jones sailed for France in the *Ranger*, his largest ship yet. Once in France, he was supposed to take command of the *L'Indien*. Jones must have been elated. He was finally getting what he wanted—command of a large ship and the prestige and respect that came with it.

During the voyage, Jones and the crew of the *Ranger* captured two British merchant ships. They escorted the ships to Paris, where Jones met Benjamin Franklin, the American ambassador to France. Franklin took the Scottish captain under his wing and introduced him to Louis XVI's court.

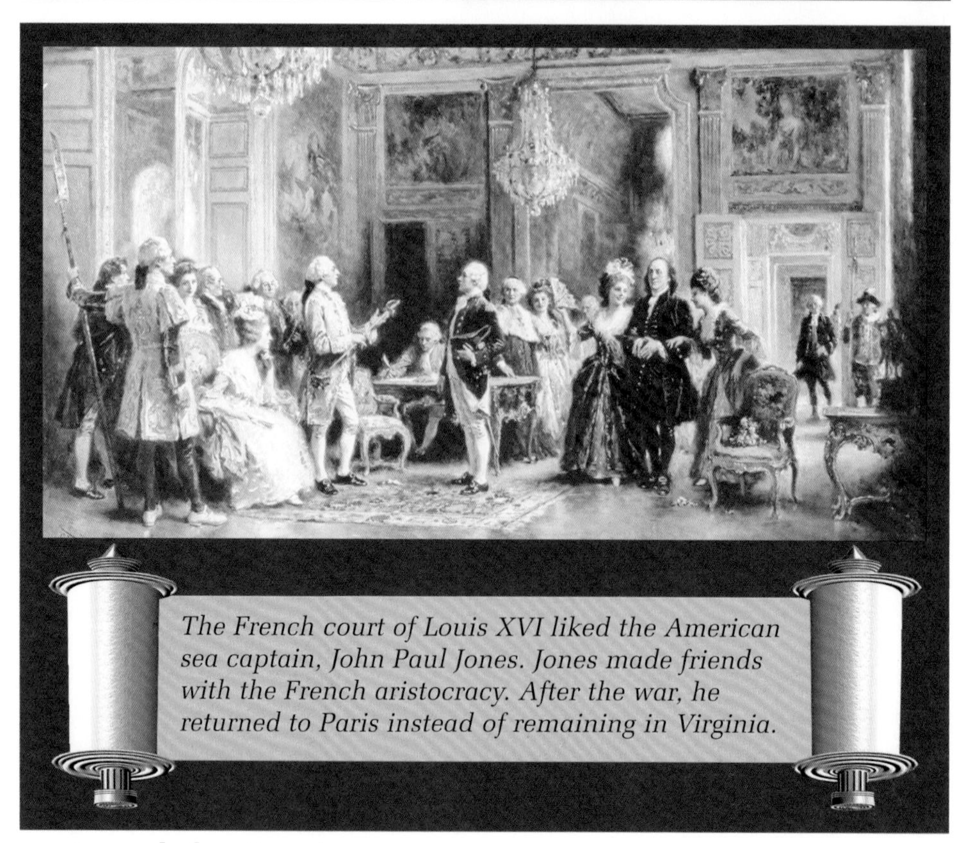

*The French court of Louis XVI liked the American sea captain, John Paul Jones. Jones made friends with the French aristocracy. After the war, he returned to Paris instead of remaining in Virginia.*

Toward the French aristocracy, Jones was polite and modest. Members of the French court treated him to intimate dinners, lavish parties, and the theater. Congress and the Marine Committee wouldn't have recognized their surly, know-it-all sea captain.

The captain's Paris vacation ended abruptly when Congress decided they couldn't pay for the new ship they'd promised him. Disappointed, he headed for the British Isles. He meant to terrorize British citizens on their own soil.

In April of 1778, the *Ranger* anchored for the night in Whitehaven, a small English port. Jones intended to burn the village and its fishing boats. The crew mutinied. They objected to burning ships that they could capture for prize money. Some historians credit the crew with objecting to burning homes, but it's more likely that they were thinking of the lost prize money. It's doubtful that they felt compassion for the villagers. On the other hand, Jones knew that an attack on English soil would devastate British morale.

Jones held a loaded pistol to the head of David Cullam, the mutiny's leader. That put an end to the crew's objections.

At dawn on April 23, a raiding party landed. Jones led a group over the fort's walls. They took a few prisoners and sabotaged the fort's guns.

Initially, Jones had the upper hand, but the raid failed. A member of the crew ran through the streets banging on doors and yelling to wake up the villagers. The raiders retreated to the ship. Jones later wrote of the attempted raid:

> What was done . . . is sufficient to show that not all their boasted navy can protect their own shore, and that the scenes of distress which they have occasioned in America may be soon brought home to their own door. . . . I was pleased that in this business we neither killed nor wounded any person.[1]

Immediately, the crew set sail for St. Mary's Isle. Jones planned to kidnap the Earl of Selkirk—the same earl who had employed both of his parents during his childhood. Surely the British government would pay a fair ransom for the earl, Jones thought. In truth, it's doubtful that the British government would have paid anything for the insignificant earl.

Jones took a few men inland, where they walked to the estate. It was still morning and the family was at breakfast. The earl's wife saw the men lurking outside and invited them in. She didn't know who they were. Once in the house, the men learned that the earl was away on business. With no earl to kidnap, they stole the family's silver, including the teapot from the breakfast table.

Traveling south from Scotland, they encountered the *Drake* on April 24. The British captain thought the *Ranger* was a merchant ship and signaled for identification. Jones didn't respond. Then the British captain sent an officer over to identify the ship. After allowing the British officer to board his ship, Captain Jones told him that he was a prisoner of Captain John Paul Jones of the United States Navy.

Soon, the *Drake* raised English colors and the *Ranger* raised the Stars and Stripes—the new United States flag. Tradition holds that Jones was the first to fly the Stars and Stripes on a navy vessel, years earlier on the *Alfred*. Since we know this only from Captain Jones's writings, there is no way to determine whether it is true. Nor do we

*The British warship the* Drake *quickly fell to Captain Jones aboard the* Ranger. *British casualties were high.*

know which flag he flew. When the *Drake* hailed the *Ranger*, the British officer identified the ship as the American Continental ship *Ranger*.

The battle was short, and we don't know many details about the fight. We do know that the captain of the *Drake* died and several of his officers suffered serious wounds. Most likely, with their leadership unable to continue, the crew surrendered.

The *Ranger* escorted its latest prize to Brest, France. Arriving on May 8, Jones found he was famous. He had raided England, and captured two merchant ships and a British man-of-war. The British authorities were furious that he had invaded their island and terrorized its citizens. More devastating than the infamous raid on Whitehaven was his capture of the *Drake*—Jones had seized a British naval vessel in their territorial waters.

Many historians credit Jones with capturing the first British naval vessel in British territory. In fact, a privateer, the *Cromwell*, captured the British *Lynx* on June 7, 1777. The battle for the *Drake*

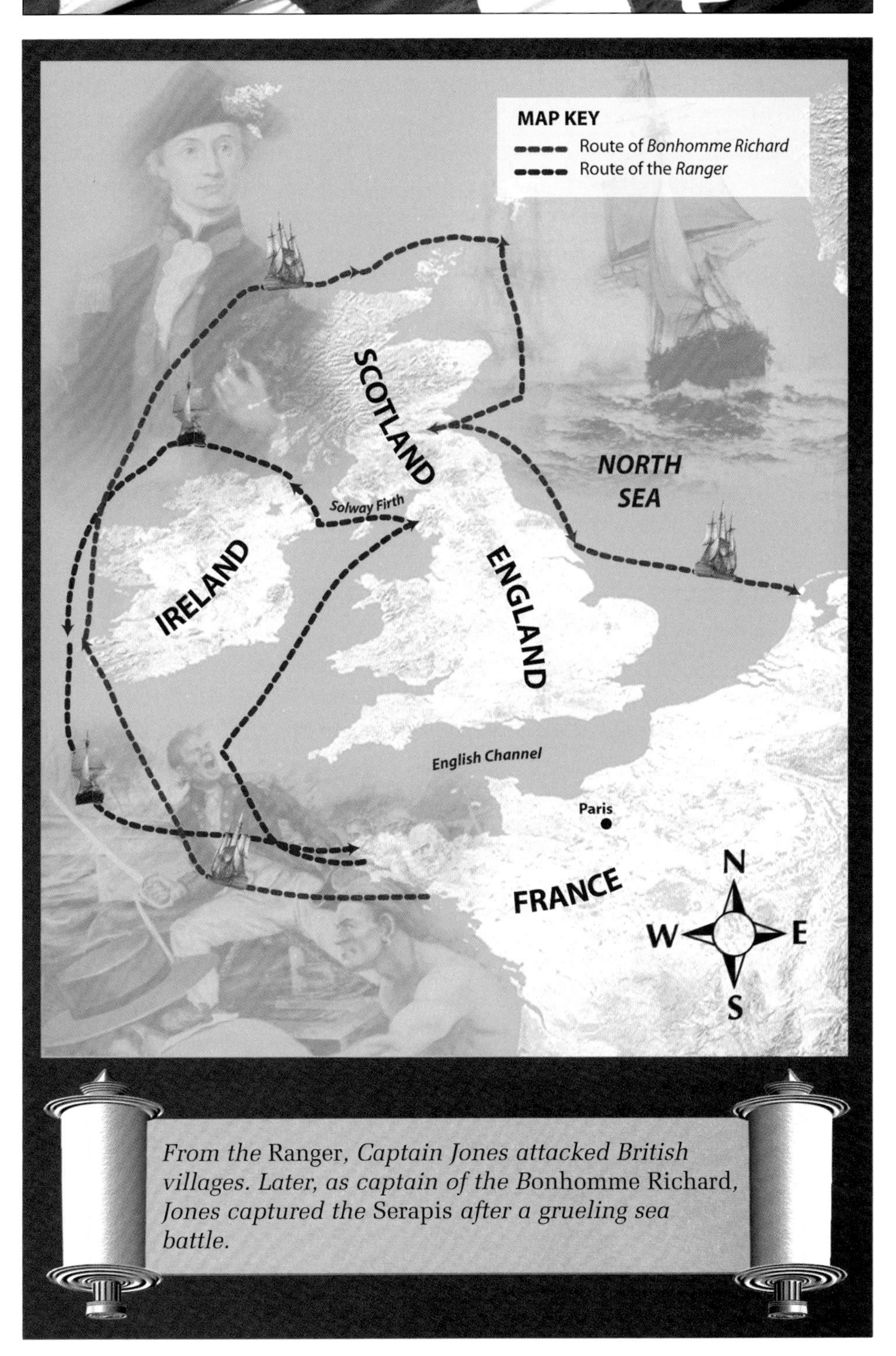


*From the* Ranger, *Captain Jones attacked British villages. Later, as captain of the* Bonhomme Richard, *Jones captured the* Serapis *after a grueling sea battle.*

was one of the most important captures to date, even if it wasn't the first. The *London Morning Chronicle* reported the event on May 9, 1778: "[In] engagements with the French and Spaniards such a superiority would have been laughed at; but the case is different when we engage with our own countrymen; men who have the same spirit and bravery with ourselves."[2]

Responding to the news of the *Drake*, forty thousand Irishmen joined the American armed forces.

Jones, feeling remorseful for his behavior in Scotland, wrote a letter of apology to Lady Selkirk. He even returned the silver after the war and paid $510 to the crew for compensation.

Jones remained in France through the summer of 1779, when King Louis XVI put him in charge of a French ship, the *Duc de Duras*. Jones renamed her *Bonhomme Richard*, after Benjamin Franklin. Translated, *Bonhomme Richard* means "Poor Richard," a reference to Franklin's famous *Poor Richard's Almanack*.

Jones outfitted the ship with forty guns. He chose an experienced and disciplined crew.

On August 14, 1779, Commodore Jones sailed his new ship out to sea with four other war vessels. The small squadron was under his command. Jones seized several British ships and sent them back to France. The fleet was doing well. However, Jones did have one problem. Captain Landais of the *Alliance* was often violent, always suspicious, and refused to obey orders.

After a long career in the French navy, Captain Landais had convinced Congress to give him a commission in the Continental Navy. While in Massachusetts, Samuel Adams persuaded the General Court at Boston to make Landais an honorary citizen of Massachusetts. There's some speculation that Adams hoped to replace Jones with Landais. John Adams spent some time on board the *Alliance* and wrote of Landias in his diary: "[He] is jealous of every Thing, jealous of every Body, of all his officers, all his Passengers; he knows not how to treat his officers, nor his passengers, nor any Body else. . . . He is bewildered—an absent bewildered man—an embarrassed Mind."[3]

On September 23, 1779, Captain Jones caught sight of a British merchant convoy. The *Serapis* and the *Countess of Scarborough*, British naval ships, were escorting forty-one merchant ships.

Captain Jones was about to win one of the most spectacular naval battles of the war.

## A Ship's Colors

The term *colors* refers to a flag—specifically, to a flag that identifies a unit. The ships of the British and Continental navies all flew unique colors. It wasn't enough to fly the flag of a nation—anyone could fly any country's flag that they liked. In fact, it was a common trick to fly the flag of an enemy so they'd let down their guard.

Ships used their colors to signal their friendly intent to one another, and to avoid being mistaken for pirates. Colonial ships usually flew their colony's flag.

Supposedly, the *Alfred* commissioned a new ensign with thirteen red and white stripes (shown on page 22). Each stripe represented one of the thirteen colonies. The canton in the upper left corner combined the crosses of St. Andrew and St. George. These crosses had appeared on the British flag since 1707, when England and Scotland united. Displaying the canton of crosses showed that the colonies still thought of themselves as English subjects.

*Jones shoots a man who had attempted to strike his colours*

Jones claimed to be the first to fly the new Stars and Stripes of the United States on December 3, 1775: "I hoisted with my own hands the flag of freedom."[4]

He was serving onboard the *Alfred*, docked in Philadelphia at the time. He claimed that citizens on shore cheered the new flag. There's no way to know if his claim is true, but the story has become folklore.

George Washington gets credit for raising the flag next, on January 1, 1776, during the siege of Boston.

Eventually, they replaced the canton of crosses with thirteen white stars on a blue field. Congress adopted the field of stars and the red and white stripes in June of 1777.

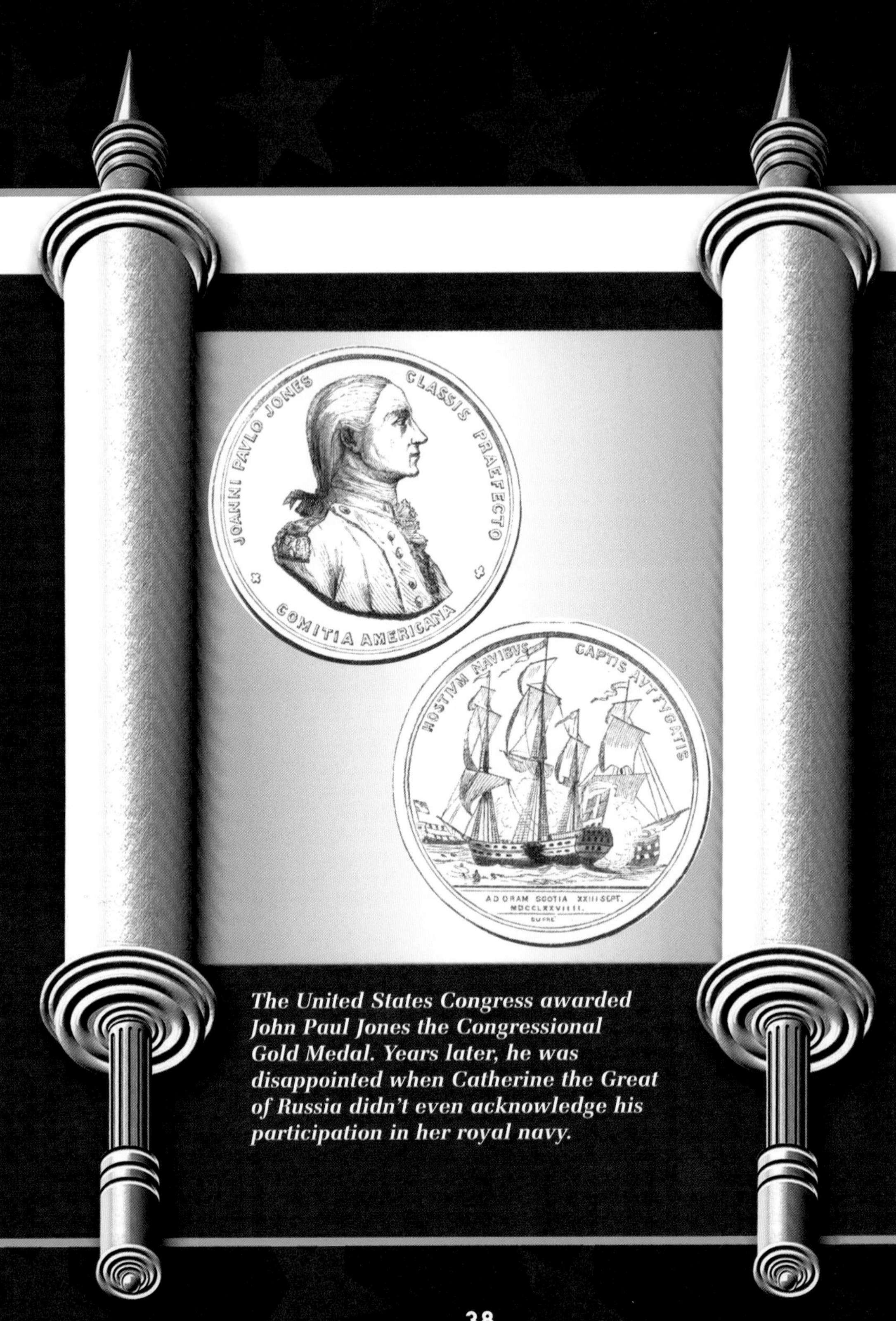


*The United States Congress awarded John Paul Jones the Congressional Gold Medal. Years later, he was disappointed when Catherine the Great of Russia didn't even acknowledge his participation in her royal navy.*

# CHAPTER 5

## After the Glory

Jones returned to America in early 1781, but most of the navy vessels were gone—either captured by the British or destroyed. After declaring peace in September of 1783, Congress sent Jones to France. He spent the next three years trying to recover prize money due to American seamen from the French government.

Life was good in Paris. The people treated Jones as a war hero. However, the French authorities were slow to turn over the prize money.

At the age of forty-one, Jones returned to the United States with funds from the French government. Although the American Congress presented him with the Congressional Gold Medal in October of 1787, he decided to retire in Paris. He was the only member of the United States Navy to receive that medal for his participation in the Revolutionary War.

Meanwhile, the French Revolution was simmering. Farther east, Catherine II, Empress of Russia, was expanding her territory.

Catherine's goal was to add Constantinople (now Istanbul) in Turkey to the Russian empire. She knew Jones by reputation, and several people suggested that she hire him to command her fleet in the Black Sea. Eventually, Thomas Jefferson recommended Jones to the Russian minister. When the minister let the empress know that

Jones was available and interested, she exclaimed, "Jones will get to Constantinople!"[1]

She hired Jones to command the fleet. His title was Rear Admiral in the Imperial Russian Navy. They called him Kontradmiral Pavel Ivanovich, which means Paul, the son of John.

During that time, it was common for a naval officer to serve in another country during times of peace. At least twenty British naval officers joined the Russian navy around the same time. They weren't happy with the appointment of Jones, and they tried to force the Russian officials to withdraw their offer.

Jones arrived in St. Petersburg on May 4, 1788 (April 23 by the Russian calendar). During his first meeting with the empress, she discussed the American Revolution. She predicted that the revolution would have a global impact: ". . . the American Revolution cannot fail to bring about others and to influence every other government."[2]

France was already on the cusp of revolution. Russia wouldn't see revolution for another hundred years, but it would come.

There was a misunderstanding as to Jones's actual position in the Russian Navy. He believed he was to command the entire fleet in the Black Sea. However, Prince Grigori Aleksandrovich Potemkin, commander in chief of all the armed forces, had a different plan.

On June 9, Rear Admiral Jones took command of his squadron in the Black Sea: the flagship *Vladimir*, eight frigates, and four other vessels. Also sailing in the Black Sea was a group of small amphibious boats called the Flotilla, under the command of another rear admiral, the Prince of Nassau-Siegen. Although Jones thought the prince courageous and self-confident, he didn't respect the prince's abilities to lead. Both admirals reported to Potemkin, making them equal in rank.

By mid-June, the Turkish fleet was moving toward Russian waters with the intention of sinking their entire fleet. The Russians were outnumbered, two to one, but luck was with them: The Turkish flagship ran aground. The remaining ships waited nearby. Nassau-Siegen wanted to attack immediately, but Jones convinced him to wait.

That evening, Jones spent several hours in a small rowboat with a Russian Cossack named Ivan. Under the guise of bringing salt to the Turkish flagship, Ivan and the admiral (in disguise) rowed between

the anchored Turkish vessels. Twice Turkish Cossacks stopped them, but Ivan had no trouble persuading them of the importance of their salt run.

Today, we would say the admiral was gathering intelligence. He was so bold and confident that across the stern of one large Turkish gunboat he wrote in French, "To be burned. Paul Jones."[3]

He made good on the threat, too—he burned the ship the next morning in battle. In two days of fighting, the Turks lost fifteen ships. The Russians took 1,673 Turkish prisoners, and 3,000 Turks died. Russian losses were few. They lost only one vessel and eighteen men.

Nassau-Siegen took full credit for the victory, completely ignoring the fact that it had been Jones's idea to wait and gather information about the enemy fleet. Later, when Catherine rewarded the officers with medals and other honors, Jones received nothing.

Jones won the respect and loyalty of most of the Russian officers who served under him, but Potemkin and Nassau-Siegen didn't like him. Potemkin's influence with the empress was absolute, and soon Jones was out of favor. On October 31, 1788, Jones was relieved of his command. Catherine never recalled him to duty, although Jones waited in Russia for several months.

Jones was a bitter man when he returned to Paris in May of 1790. He was low on funds and friends.

He spent his last two years in Paris. The old Paris of parties and the adoring aristocracy was gone—victims of the French Revolution. He had little to occupy his time.

His health was bad and getting worse. He was unable to return to sea. Although he received a few invitations to visit old friends, he was unable to travel. Mostly, he stayed home and wrote letters.

For a short while, it appeared that fortune was again smiling on Jones. In June 1792, Congress appointed him the special American representative to the Sultan's Court at Algiers. It was a dignified position. Jones probably would have excelled as a representative. Unfortunately, the letter with the appointment didn't arrive until mid-August—almost a month after Jones died.

John Paul Jones died alone in Paris on July 18, 1792. His old friend Robert Morris found him lying facedown on his bed, with his feet on the floor. He was forty-five. Most likely, he died of pneumonia.

*In the early twentieth century, the remains of John Paul Jones were laid to rest beneath the chapel of the U.S. Naval Academy in Annapolis.*

The French loved Jones and gave him a formal funeral. A squad of uniformed soldiers marched at the head of his procession. Carriages of prominent French politicians and friends followed the soldiers. They laid the coffin to rest on July 20 in a cemetery near Paris.

His small estate of a few thousand dollars in stock and some land in Vermont went to his sisters. His friend Morris sold Jones's uniforms and medals to pay his debts.

One hundred and thirteen years later, General Horace Porter, the American ambassador to France, found the grave. In 1905, President Theodore Roosevelt sent four cruisers to France to escort the naval hero's body to the United States. With great fanfare, they reburied John Paul Jones in a naval ceremony. Several warships fired a salute for the famous sea captain. His coffin now rests in the crypt of the chapel of the United States Naval Academy at Annapolis.

The British never forgot the captain. In 1940, Britain resisted when Germany tried to invade their island. Albert Alexander, First Lord of the Admiralty, remembered Jones in a broadcast to America: "In the words of your own great seaman, Captain Paul Jones, Britain has not yet begun to fight."[4]

## About the Body

John Paul Jones died in Paris in 1792, just a few weeks before a mob of angry peasants overran the French royal palace. Pierrot François Simmoneau, a French official, assumed the Americans would want to claim Jones's body. He used his own money to pay to have the corpse placed in alcohol and then sealed in a lead coffin.

Believing Jones's family would claim his personal items, the French wrapped his body in a sheet. They didn't bury him in one of his uniforms or with any of his decorations or medals.

At the cemetery, they placed the coffin in its grave, threw in some dirt, and fired one last salute.

Three weeks later, in August 1792, a Paris mob killed Swiss guards who tried to protect the king and queen of France. Later, they dumped the guards' bodies into a common grave alongside Jones's grave. Soon after, the cemetery closed.

One hundred years later, the cemetery was covered by houses. General Horace Porter, the American ambassador to France, received permission to excavate the area. First, the excavators found the bones of the Swiss guards. Next, they unearthed two lead coffins containing the remains of unknown citizens.

*John Paul Jones's corpse*

On April 7, 1905, they opened a third lead coffin. In it they found a well-preserved corpse. An autopsy confirmed that the body was that of John Paul Jones. A report from the excavation claimed that the body in the third coffin contained "a remarkably well-preserved corpse whose face had an unmistakable resemblance to the portrait of John Paul Jones."[5]

Eight years later, his body was brought to Annapolis.

## Chronology

**1747** John Paul is born on July 6 in the gardener's cottage of the Arbigland Estate in Kirkbean, Scotland.

**1760** At the age of thirteen, Paul becomes an apprentice to an English merchant and goes to sea.

**1767** Paul saves the *John* and receives his first command at the age of twenty-one.

**1770** Mungo Maxwell is flogged for disobeying Paul.

**1772** Paul takes command of the *Betsy*.

**1773** After killing a mutineer onboard the *Betsy*, John Paul flees to Fredericksburg, Virginia, and takes charge of his recently deceased brother's estate. He also adds the name Jones.

**1775** Jones receives his commission as first lieutenant in the Continental Navy. He is the first to fly the Stars and Stripes, according to his writings.

**1776** Jones takes command of the *Providence*; then sails for France in the *Ranger*.

**1778** He leads a raid against Whitehaven, England, on April 23. The next day, he captures the *Drake* in British waters.

**1779** Command of the *Bonhomme Richard* is awarded to Jones; the ship is renamed in honor of Benjamin Franklin and his book *Poor Richard's Almanack*. In September, Jones engages and captures the *Serapis* in a battle that convinces the French to support the American colonies in their struggle to cast off British rule.

**1783** Jones returns to Paris to negotiate prize money claims for American seamen.

**1787** The Congressional Gold Medal is awarded to Jones.

**1788** He takes command of the Black Sea fleet for Empress Catherine II of Russia as a rear admiral.

**1790** Jones arrives in Paris, where he remains in retirement despite his attempts to be recalled to the Russian navy.

**1792** In June, Jones is appointed special American representative to the Sultan's Court at Algiers, where he is to work for the release of American captives. On July 18, before he can undertake the role, Jones dies.

**1905** Jones's remains are identified by General Horace Porter, the U.S. Ambassador to France. Porter had spent six years trying to locate the grave.

**1913** After being given a hero's procession by U.S. cruisers and battleships, Jones is reburied in the chapel of the United States Naval Academy at Annapolis, Maryland, in a ceremony presided over by President Theodore Roosevelt.

## Timeline in History

**1696** Navigation laws mandate that all trade between colonies and England must be transported in English-built ships.
**1754** The French and Indian War begins on American soil.
**1763** The French and Indian War ends.
**1764** Parliament passes the Sugar Act.
**1765** Parliament passes the Stamp Act.
**1766** Parliament repeals the Stamp Act. Parliament passes the Declaratory Act, which states that Parliament has the power to make all laws for Americans.
**1773** Patriots organize the Boston Tea Party.
**1774** The First Continental Congress convenes in Philadelphia.
**1775** Patrick Henry gives his famous "Give me liberty or give me death" speech at the Second Virginia Convention. The Revolutionary War begins with the battles of Concord and Bunker Hill.
**1776** The Continental Navy fleet heads for sea. The Declaration of Independence is adopted.
**1781** Cornwallis surrenders at Yorktown, ending the war.
**1789** The U.S. Constitution is ratified. The French Revolution begins. George Washington becomes the first president of the United States.
**1803** The United States buys Louisiana from the French.
**1812** The British burn the White House in Washington, D.C., in the War of 1812.
**1844** Samuel Morse sends the first telegraph message from Baltimore to Washington.

# Chapter Notes

### Chapter 1 A Moonlit Victory

1. John Evangelist Walsh, *Night on Fire: The First Complete Account of John Paul Jones's Greatest Battle* (New York: McGraw-Hill Book Company, 1978), pp. 81–82.
2. Evan Thomas, *John Paul Jones: Sailor, Hero, Father of the American Navy* (New York: Simon & Schuster, 2003), p. 192.

### Chapter 2 Childhood Adventures, Troubles, and a Mystery

1. Lincoln Lorenz, *John Paul Jones: Fighter for Freedom and Glory* (Annapolis: the United States Naval Institute, 1943), p. 13.
2. Ibid., p. 26.
3. Evan Thomas, *John Paul Jones: Sailor, Hero, Father of the American Navy* (New York: Simon & Schuster, 2003), pp. 39–40
4. Ibid., p. 40.

### Chapter 3 A Revolutionary Sea Captain

1. Evan Thomas, *John Paul Jones: Sailor, Hero, Father of the American Navy* (New York: Simon & Schuster, 2003), p. 46.

### Chapter 4 In Enemy Waters

1. Lincoln Lorenz, *John Paul Jones: Fighter for Freedom and Glory* (Annapolis: United States Naval Institute, 1943), p. 147.
2. Samuel Eliot Morison, *John Paul Jones: A Sailor's Biography* (Boston: Little, Brown and Company, 1959), p. 161.
3. Ibid., p. 190.
4. Barbara W. Tuchman, *The First Salute* (New York: Alfred A. Knopf, 1988), p. 48.

### Chapter 5 After the Glory

1. Samuel Eliot Morison, *John Paul Jones: A Sailor's Biography* (Boston: Little, Brown & Company, 1959), p. 362.
2. Ibid., p. 364.
3. Ibid., p. 377.
4. Ibid., p. 413.
5. Mike Wright, *What They Didn't Teach You About the American Revolution* (Novato, Calif.: Presidio Press, 1999), p. 310.

# Further Reading


### For Young Adults

Callo, Joseph F. *John Paul Jones: America's First Sea Warrior.* Annapolis, Maryland: Naval Institute Press, 2006.

Cooper, Michael. *Hero of the High Seas: John Paul Jones and the American Revolution.* Washington, D.C.: National Geographic Children's Books, 2006.

Hossell, Karen Price. *John Paul Jones.* Chicago: Heinemann Library, 2004.

Sperry, Armstrong. *John Paul Jones: The Pirate Patriot.* New York: Sterling Point Books, 2006.

### Works Consulted

De Koven, Anna Farwell. *The Life and Letters of John Paul Jones.* New York: Charles Scribner's Sons, 1913.

Evan, Thomas. *John Paul Jones: Sailor, Hero, Father of the American Navy.* New York: Simon & Schuster, 2003.

Lorenz, Lincoln. *John Paul Jones: Fighter for Freedom and Glory.* Annapolis, Maryland: The United States Naval Institute, 1943.

Morison, Samuel Eliot. *John Paul Jones: A Sailor's Biography, 1959.* Boston: Little, Brown & Company, 1959.

Tuchman, Barbara W. *The First Salute.* New York: Alfred A. Knopf, 1988.

Walsh, John Evangelist. *Night on Fire: The First Complete Account of John Paul Jones's Greatest Battle.* New York: McGraw-Hill, 1978.

Wright, Mike. *What They Didn't Teach You About the American Revolution.* Novato, California: Presidio Press, 1999.

### On the Internet

John Paul Jones Cottage Museum. http://www.jpj.demon.co.uk/

"I have not yet begun to fight": The Story of John Paul Jones. Naval Historical Center. http://www.history.navy.mil/trivia/trivia02a.htm

250th Anniversary of the Birth of John Paul Jones. Naval Historical Center. http://www.history.navy.mil/faqs/faq58-1.htm

Kenneth J. Hagan; James C. Bradford (contributing); Lincoln Lorenz (contributing). "John Paul Jones: Father of the American Navy." The American Revolution Home Page. http://www.americanrevwar.homestead.com/files/JONES.HTM

USS John Paul Jones. http://www.john-paul-jones.navy.mil/

AmericanRevolution.org. http://www.americanrevolution.org/jpj.html

John Paul Jones Park. New York City Department of Parks and Recreation. http://www.nycgovparks.org/sub_your_park/historical_signs/hs_historical_sign.php?id=11908

# Index